RETENTION STRATEGIES

Cultivating a Loyal and Productive Workforce

Juan D. Huerta M.B.A, PHR

This book is dedicated to my for Huerta girls, thank you for keeping me grounded to what trully matters in life.

CONTENTS

Success

FOREWORD

Welcome to Retention Strategies: Cultivating a Loyal and Productive Workforce. In the dynamic and competitive landscape of today's business world, the key to success lies not just in attracting top talent but also in retaining that talent for the long haul. Employee retention is not a mere buzzword; it is the cornerstone of a thriving and sustainable organization.

This book is your ultimate guide to understanding the significance of employee retention and unlocking the secrets to building an engaged and committed workforce. Whether you are an HR professional seeking comprehensive strategies or a business leader looking to foster a culture of loyalty and productivity, this book will equip you with the tools and insights you need.

PREFACE

In the opening chapters, we will delve into the implications of high employee turnover and the substantial costs it imposes on organizations. Recognizing this, we will then move on to explore how to establish a strong organizational culture that aligns with your company's mission, values, and goals. The subsequent chapters will focus on various retention strategies that you can implement to reduce turnover and create an environment where employees feel valued, supported, and invested in their roles.Throughout this book, we will emphasize the critical role of leadership in retaining talent and highlight persuasive case studies of companies that have excelled in employee retention. Drawing from real-world experiences, backed by extensive research, each chapter will provide actionable steps and proven practices to strengthen your retention efforts.

Remember, employee retention is not just a matter of financial gains; it is about nurturing a sense of belonging and purpose within your workforce. The journey to fostering loyalty and commitment begins here.

CHAPTER 1: UNDERSTANDING THE IMPORTANCE OF EMPLOYEE RETENTION

In the ever-changing landscape of business, employee retention has emerged as a fundamental factor in an organization's success. Gone are the days when employees stayed with a company for decades; today, the job market is marked by mobility and the pursuit of new opportunities. In this chapter, we will explore why employee retention matters and how it impacts various aspects of your organization.

At the heart of a successful business lies a dedicated and competent workforce. Employee retention directly influences productivity, efficiency, and ultimately, the bottom line. High turnover disrupts workflow, derails projects, and hampers team dynamics, whereas a stable and committed workforce fosters creativity, innovation, and a harmonious work environment.

The costs associated with employee turnover are staggering. Beyond the tangible expenses of recruitment, onboarding, and training, there are intangible costs such as the loss of institutional knowledge, reduced team morale, and decreased customer satisfaction. Furthermore, high turnover tarnishes a company's reputation, making it less attractive to potential candidates and customers alike.

Throughout this chapter, we will delve into the intricacies of measuring employee turnover and calculating its impact on your organization. By understanding the true cost of losing employees, you will gain valuable insights that will underscore the importance of prioritizing retention strategies.

In subsequent chapters, we will explore various techniques that organizations can employ to retain their talent effectively. From fostering a positive work culture to providing competitive compensation and meaningful recognition, each strategy will play a pivotal role in strengthening your workforce's loyalty and commitment.

As you embark on this journey to create a loyal and engaged workforce, remember that investing in employee retention is an investment in the future of your organization. The benefits will extend far beyond the bottom line, as you build a thriving and enduring company that attracts and retains top talent in the industry.

CHAPTER 2: ANALYZING THE COSTS OF HIGH EMPLOYEE TURNOVER

In Chapter 1, we explored the significance of employee retention as the bedrock of a thriving organization. Now, let us delve deeper into the specific costs incurred due to high employee turnover. Understanding these costs is essential to grasp the urgency of implementing effective retention strategies.

Recruitment Expenses: The process of replacing a departing employee involves advertising, screening, interviewing, and selecting candidates. Each step incurs expenses, from posting job listings on various platforms to conducting background checks and assessments. High turnover means frequently repeating this costly process.

Onboarding and Training Costs: When a new employee joins the organization, they require training and onboarding to become productive contributors. Skilled trainers, training materials, and dedicated time from current employees all represent significant investments.

Loss of Productivity: As a new employee gets acclimated to the job, their productivity may be lower than that of an experienced employee. This productivity gap can translate into missed opportunities, delayed projects, and decreased overall efficiency.

Impact on Team Morale: Frequent turnover disrupts team dynamics and creates an air of uncertainty among remaining employees. The departure of a colleague can lead to decreased morale and negatively affect the team's cohesion and motivation.

Loss of Institutional Knowledge: Experienced employees possess valuable knowledge about the company's operations, culture, and processes. When they leave, this institutional knowledge leaves with them, and the organization must work to fill the gap.

Customer Satisfaction: High employee turnover can lead to inconsistent customer service, affecting customer satisfaction and loyalty. Satisfied customers are the lifeblood of any business, and losing them due to poor service can be detrimental.

Time Invested in Development: Organizations invest considerable time and resources in developing their employees' skills. When employees leave, the investment made in their development may not yield the expected returns.

Impact on Company Reputation: A high employee turnover rate can tarnish an organization's reputation in the job market. Potential candidates may perceive the company as unstable or lacking opportunities for growth, making it challenging to attract top talent.

Reduced Employee Engagement: Constantly seeing colleagues leave can demotivate remaining employees, leading to reduced engagement and dedication to their roles.

Opportunity Cost: The time and resources spent on recruitment and training could have been allocated to initiatives that drive innovation and growth. High turnover drains valuable resources that could otherwise be invested in the company's strategic priorities.

In light of these compelling costs, it becomes evident that reducing employee turnover is not just a matter of HR concern; it is a business imperative. The investment in retaining talent pays dividends in terms of enhanced productivity, improved morale, and a positive corporate image.

By addressing the root causes of turnover and implementing comprehensive retention strategies, you can create an environment where employees feel valued, supported, and motivated to contribute their best. In the following chapters, we will equip you with actionable techniques and proven practices to build a strong foundation for retaining your most valuable asset— your people.

Remember, it is within your power to reverse the tide of turnover and foster a loyal, engaged, and high-performing workforce. Your organization's success and competitiveness depend on it. Let us embark on this journey together, as we unlock the secrets to cultivating a loyal and productive workforce that will drive your organization to new heights of success.

CHAPTER 3:
BUILDING A STRONG
ORGANIZATIONAL
CULTURE

In Chapter 2, we delved into the costs of high employee turnover, highlighting the urgent need for effective retention strategies. One of the most potent tools in your arsenal is to build a strong organizational culture that fosters loyalty and commitment among your employees. A robust culture is not just a buzzword; it is the guiding force that shapes attitudes, behaviors, and the overall employee experience within your company.

Why Organizational Culture Matters:

Organizational culture is the collective personality of your company. It sets the tone for how employees interact with one another, with leadership, and with customers. A positive culture promotes shared values, a sense of purpose, and a strong sense of belonging. When employees feel a deep connection to the organization's mission and values, they are more likely to stay engaged, committed, and enthusiastic about their work.

Aligning Culture with Core Values:

To build a strong organizational culture, start by defining your company's core values and aligning them with every aspect of your operations. Your core values should reflect what your organization stands for, what it aims to achieve, and the principles that guide decision-making. When these values permeate your culture, employees feel a genuine connection to the organization's purpose.

Fostering Open Communication:

Clear and open communication is the lifeblood of a thriving culture. Encourage transparency at all levels of the

2 / 2

CHAPTER 4:
RECRUITING THE
RIGHT TALENT
FROM THE START

I n Chapter 3, we emphasized the significance of building a strong organizational culture as a cornerstone of employee retention. Now, we shift our focus to the pivotal role of effective recruitment in laying the foundation for a loyal and productive workforce. Attracting and selecting the right talent from the start sets the stage for a successful and enduring employer-employee relationship.

The Power of Strategic Recruitment:

Strategic recruitment is more than just filling vacancies; it is a deliberate and purposeful process aimed at identifying candidates who not only possess the right skills but also align with your company's values and culture. These candidates are more likely to become engaged employees who stay committed to the organization for the long haul.

Crafting Compelling Job Descriptions:

Start your recruitment process with a clear and compelling job description that accurately outlines the role's responsibilities and expectations. Be specific about the required skills and qualifications, but also highlight the company's mission, culture, and the opportunities for growth that await the successful candidate.

Leveraging Employer Branding:

Your employer brand is the perception that current and potential employees have of your organization as an employer. A positive and well-defined employer brand attracts top talent and instills a sense of pride and loyalty among existing employees. Showcase your company's unique selling points, employee benefits, and success stories to create an irresistible employer brand.

Tapping into Talent Networks:

Explore various avenues to connect with potential candidates, including talent networks, industry events, and social media platforms. Engage in proactive talent sourcing to identify passive candidates who might not be actively seeking new opportunities but could be a perfect fit for your organization.

Streamlining the Selection Process:

A prolonged and convoluted selection process can deter qualified candidates and lead to losing them to competitors. Streamline your hiring process without compromising on due diligence. Establish clear timelines, communicate regularly with candidates, and involve key stakeholders to make timely decisions.

Conducting Behavior-Based Interviews:

Traditional interviews often focus on hypothetical scenarios, while behavior-based interviews delve into a candidate's past experiences and behaviors. Such interviews provide valuable insights into how candidates handle challenges and align with your company's values, making it easier to identify those who will thrive in your organization's culture.

**Engaging with

2 / 2

, and engaging. Candidates form impressions of your organization based on their recruitment experience, so treat each interaction as an opportunity to showcase your company's professionalism and commitment to its employees.

Offering Competitive Compensation and Benefits:

Attracting the right talent requires offering competitive compensation packages and attractive benefits. Research industry standards and ensure that your remuneration aligns with the skills and experience of the candidates you seek. Additionally, consider offering unique perks and incentives that set your organization apart from competitors.

Highlighting Career Development Opportunities:

Top candidates are not only seeking a job but also a fulfilling career path. Emphasize the opportunities for growth and development within your organization. Showcase success stories of employees who have progressed within the company, and outline the support and resources available for employees to enhance their skills and climb the career ladder.

Engaging in Diversity and Inclusion Efforts:

A diverse and inclusive workforce contributes to a thriving organizational culture and boosts employee retention. Demonstrate your commitment to diversity and inclusion through targeted recruitment efforts and inclusive language in job postings. Highlight initiatives that promote a sense of belonging for all employees, regardless of their background.

Sealing the Deal with Onboarding Excellence:

Once you have identified the right candidates, an exceptional onboarding process sets the tone for a successful tenure. Make new employees feel welcomed, valued, and prepared for their roles. A well-structured onboarding program introduces them to the company's culture, values, and colleagues, fostering a positive and lasting impression.

Supporting Managers in Their Role:

Managers play a critical role in employee retention. Provide them with the necessary training and resources to effectively lead and support their teams. Encourage open communication between managers and employees, allowing for feedback, mentorship, and professional development discussions.

Measuring Recruitment Success:

To continuously improve your recruitment efforts, establish key performance indicators (KPIs) to measure the effectiveness of your hiring process. Track metrics such as time-to-fill, candidate satisfaction, and employee retention rates to identify areas for enhancement and celebrate successes.

By adopting a strategic and people-centered approach to recruitment, you create a strong pipeline of talent that aligns with your organization's mission, values, and culture. The right candidates are not just skilled; they are individuals who embrace your company's vision and are eager to contribute to its success. As they become part of a positive and engaging work environment, they are more likely to remain loyal, committed, and invested in your organization's journey toward greatness.

In the next chapter, we will explore the essential role of effective onboarding programs in nurturing new employees and integrating them seamlessly into your organizational culture. The onboarding process is not merely a formality; it is a crucial opportunity to lay the groundwork for a long and fruitful relationship with your talent. Let us continue our journey to unlocking the secrets of employee retention together.

CHAPTER 5: IMPLEMENTING EFFECTIVE ONBOARDING PROGRAMS

I n Chapter 4, we emphasized the significance of attracting the right talent through strategic recruitment. Now, let us explore the pivotal role of effective onboarding programs in nurturing and integrating new employees seamlessly into your organizational culture. A well-designed onboarding process is not just a checkbox; it is a powerful tool that sets the stage for long-term employee engagement and retention.

The Power of Onboarding Excellence:

Effective onboarding goes beyond paperwork and orientation sessions. It is a deliberate and immersive experience that acclimates new employees to your company's values, culture, and expectations. By providing the right support and resources from day one, you set the foundation for a successful and enduring employment journey.

Crafting a Comprehensive Onboarding Plan:

Begin the onboarding process well before the employee's start date. Prepare a comprehensive onboarding plan that outlines the activities, training, and introductions they will receive during their first weeks. Personalize the plan to suit each employee's role and needs, ensuring they feel valued and welcome from the outset.

Introducing Organizational Culture and Values:

Onboarding is an ideal opportunity to introduce new employees to your company's mission, values, and vision. Demonstrate how these core principles translate into day-to-day operations and encourage employees to embrace them in their work. A strong alignment with the organization's values fosters a sense of purpose and connection.

Facilitating Relationships and Connections:

A key aspect of onboarding is helping new employees build relationships within the organization. Facilitate introductions to colleagues, team members, and leadership. Encourage mentorship and buddy programs to provide a support system and foster a sense of camaraderie.

Providing Role Clarity and Expectations:

Clearly communicate the roles and responsibilities of new employees and set expectations for performance and behavior. Provide them with the necessary tools, resources, and training to excel in their roles and contribute to the organization's success.

Emphasizing Career Development:

During onboarding, showcase the opportunities for career growth and development within your organization. Demonstrate your commitment to employee growth through training programs, workshops, and advancement paths. This emphasis on professional growth encourages long-term commitment to the company.

Engaging New Employees from the Start:

Ensure that new employees feel engaged and motivated from their first day. Involve them in meaningful projects, encourage their input, and seek their feedback on their onboarding experience. A sense of involvement and contribution right from the beginning will make them feel like integral members of the team.

Continuous Support and Check-Ins:

Onboarding should not be a one-time event; it should be a continuous process that spans the employee's first few months. Schedule regular check-ins to gauge their progress, address any concerns, and offer ongoing support. These touchpoints demonstrate your investment in their success and well-being.

Measuring Onboarding Success:

Track the effectiveness of your onboarding programs by gathering feedback from new employees and their managers. Analyze metrics such as time-to-productivity, early attrition rates, and employee satisfaction to identify areas of improvement and celebrate successes.

Remember, effective onboarding is more than just a formality; it is a crucial opportunity to integrate new employees into your organization's fabric. When employees feel valued, engaged, and connected to your company's culture from the outset, they are more likely to become loyal, committed, and passionate contributors to your organization's success.

In the next chapter, we will explore the essential role of

nurturing employee development and growth. A commitment to continuous learning and professional advancement is a powerful retention strategy that empowers employees to excel and evolve within your organization. Let us continue our journey to unlocking the secrets of employee retention together.

CHAPTER 6: NURTURING EMPLOYEE DEVELOPMENT AND GROWTH

In Chapter 5, we emphasized the significance of effective onboarding as a crucial step in fostering employee engagement and retention. Now, we delve into the essential role of nurturing employee development and growth as a powerful strategy to cultivate a loyal and high-performing workforce. When employees feel supported and invested in their professional growth, they are more likely to remain committed and motivated to contribute their best to your organization.

The Impact of Continuous Learning:

A commitment to continuous learning is not just a personal development goal; it is a strategic imperative for organizations seeking to thrive in a dynamic business landscape. When you provide opportunities for employees to enhance their skills and knowledge, they feel valued, empowered, and equipped to tackle new challenges.

Investing in Training and Development:

Offer a wide range of training and development programs that align with both individual and organizational needs. These programs may include technical skills training, leadership development, communication workshops, and more. Tailor the offerings to cater to different learning styles and career aspirations.

Encouraging Career Pathing and Advancement:

Empower employees to envision and pursue their career paths within your organization. Provide clear guidance on potential career trajectories and the skills needed to progress. When employees see a clear path for growth and advancement, they are more likely to remain committed and loyal to the organization.

Supporting Individual Development Plans:

Collaborate with employees to create personalized development plans that align with their aspirations and performance goals. These plans should be dynamic and adaptable, allowing for adjustments as employees' skills and interests evolve.

Promoting a Learning Culture:

Create a culture that values and promotes continuous learning. Encourage knowledge sharing, mentorship programs, and cross-functional training opportunities. When learning becomes an integral part of your organization's DNA, employees will feel motivated to seek new knowledge and stay engaged.

Recognizing and Rewarding Learning Achievements:

Recognize and celebrate employees' learning achievements and milestones. Whether it's completing a certification, mastering a new skill, or successfully leading a project, acknowledging their efforts and growth reinforces their commitment to self-improvement.

Embracing Technology for Learning:

Leverage technology to provide flexible and accessible learning resources. Online courses, webinars, and virtual workshops allow employees to learn at their own pace, making professional development more convenient and inclusive.

Measuring the Impact of Development Programs:

Assess the effectiveness of your development initiatives by tracking employee performance improvements, career progression rates, and employee satisfaction. Solicit feedback from participants to understand their learning experience and identify areas for enhancement.

Building a Culture of Lifelong Learning:

Fostering a culture of lifelong learning not only benefits employees but also enhances your organization's ability to adapt and innovate. As employees acquire new skills and knowledge, they become valuable assets in driving your organization's success.

Remember, employee development and growth are not just optional perks; they are investments in your organization's future. When employees experience continuous learning and see a clear path for their advancement, they are more likely to remain committed, engaged, and dedicated to your organization's mission.

In the next chapter, we will explore the importance of creating a supportive work-life balance for employees. Balancing work and personal life is crucial for well-being and job satisfaction, and organizations that prioritize employee well-being are rewarded with increased loyalty and productivity. Let us continue our journey to unlocking the secrets of employee retention together.

CHAPTER 7: CREATING A SUPPORTIVE WORK-LIFE BALANCE

In Chapter 6, we highlighted the power of nurturing employee development and growth as a key retention strategy. Now, we shift our focus to the critical aspect of creating a supportive work-life balance for employees. Striking the right balance between work and personal life is not just a trend; it is a vital component of employee well-being and job satisfaction. Organizations that prioritize the well-being of their employees are rewarded with increased loyalty, productivity, and overall satisfaction.

The Importance of Work-Life Balance:

A healthy work-life balance is not an indulgence; it is an essential foundation for a thriving and engaged workforce. When employees can fulfill their professional responsibilities while also enjoying personal time and activities, they experience reduced stress, improved mental well-being, and enhanced job satisfaction.

Promoting Flexible Work Arrangements:

Embrace flexible work arrangements, such as remote work, flextime, and compressed workweeks. These options empower employees to tailor their work schedules to better suit their personal needs and responsibilities. Trust employees to manage their time effectively, and focus on outcomes rather than hours worked.

Encouraging Time Off and Vacation Days:

Promote a culture that values time off and encourages employees to take their vacation days. Time away from work allows employees to recharge, relax, and return to work with renewed energy and focus. Encourage managers to lead by example and take time off themselves.

Supporting Employee Wellness Programs:

Invest in employee wellness programs that promote physical and mental health. Whether it's offering gym memberships, mindfulness workshops, or mental health resources, these initiatives demonstrate your commitment to employee well-being.

Setting Boundaries and Avoiding Burnout:

Encourage employees to set boundaries between work and personal life. Avoid expecting them to be constantly available outside of working hours. Recognize that sustained productivity requires well-rested and motivated employees.

Providing Parental and Caregiver Support:

Recognize the unique challenges faced by parents and caregivers in balancing their responsibilities. Offer support, such as parental leave, childcare assistance, or flexible work arrangements, to help them manage their dual roles effectively.

Recognizing and Valuing Personal Achievements:

Acknowledge and celebrate personal achievements and milestones of employees. Whether it's completing a marathon, pursuing a hobby, or attending a family event, demonstrating interest in their personal lives fosters a sense of care and appreciation.

Measuring Work-Life Balance:

Regularly assess the work-life balance of your employees through surveys and feedback sessions. Use the data to identify areas for improvement and implement policies that better support employee well-being.

Promoting a Culture of Work-Life Integration:

Encourage a culture of work-life integration, where employees feel that they can seamlessly weave their personal and professional lives together. Flexibility and understanding are the pillars of this culture.

Remember, a supportive work-life balance is not just a benefit; it is an essential aspect of creating a positive work environment where employees feel valued and cared for. By prioritizing employee well-being, you foster a sense of loyalty and commitment that extends far beyond the workplace.

In the next chapter, we will explore the significance of providing competitive compensation and benefits as a powerful retention strategy. Compensation is not just about salary; it is a statement of the value you place on your employees' contributions. Let us continue our journey to unlocking the secrets of employee retention together.

CHAPTER 8: PROVIDING COMPETITIVE COMPENSATION AND BENEFITS

In Chapter 7, we emphasized the importance of creating a supportive work-life balance for employees. Now, we turn our attention to the significant role of providing competitive compensation and benefits as a compelling retention strategy. Compensation is not merely a financial transaction; it is a reflection of the value you place on your employees' skills, expertise, and dedication. A robust compensation package, coupled with attractive benefits, is a potent combination that fosters loyalty, motivation, and commitment to your organization.

Recognizing the Value of Competitive Compensation:

Competitive compensation is the foundation of an employer-employee relationship built on mutual respect and appreciation. When employees feel that their contributions are recognized and rewarded fairly, they are more likely to remain engaged and motivated to excel.

Conducting Regular Compensation Reviews:

Stay informed about industry salary trends and conduct regular compensation reviews to ensure that your pay scales are competitive. Adjustments should be based on performance, skills, and market benchmarks, rewarding employees for their achievements and incentivizing continued growth.

Offering Performance-Based Incentives:

In addition to base compensation, consider implementing performance-based incentives to reward exceptional contributions. These incentives can take the form of bonuses, commissions, or profit-sharing programs, motivating employees to strive for excellence.

Providing Comprehensive Benefits Packages:

Beyond monetary compensation, comprehensive benefits packages play a crucial role in retaining top talent. Health insurance, retirement plans, paid time off, and other perks demonstrate your commitment to employees' well-being and quality of life.

Tailoring Benefits to Employee Needs:

Recognize that the needs of your employees may vary. Consider offering a flexible benefits program that allows employees to choose the options that best suit their individual circumstances. This customization empowers employees and shows that you value their unique needs.

Supporting Financial Wellness:

Provide resources and tools to support employees' financial wellness. Financial planning assistance, access to investment opportunities, and educational workshops can help employees make informed decisions and reduce financial stress.

Promoting Work-Life Balance Initiatives:

Integrate work-life balance initiatives into your benefits package. Offer flexible work arrangements, parental leave, remote work options, and wellness programs that contribute to employees' overall well-being.

Communicating Total Rewards:

Transparently communicate the total value of the compensation and benefits package to employees. Make sure they understand the full extent of the rewards they receive, reinforcing their sense of value to the organization.

Measuring Employee Satisfaction with Compensation:

Gather feedback from employees regarding their satisfaction with compensation and benefits. Regular surveys and discussions provide insights into their needs and allow you to make data-driven improvements.

Demonstrating Commitment to Employee Well-Being:

Competitive compensation and benefits are not just a budgetary expense; they are investments in your employees' physical, financial, and emotional well-being. By prioritizing their welfare, you create a culture where employees feel valued and appreciated.

Remember, competitive compensation and benefits are essential components of an attractive employee value proposition. By offering a rewarding and comprehensive package, you attract and retain top talent, while fostering a motivated and committed workforce.

In the next chapter, we will explore the power of recognizing and rewarding employee contributions. A culture of appreciation is a potent retention tool that empowers employees to continue giving their best to your organization. Let us continue our journey to unlocking the secrets of employee retention together.

CHAPTER 9: RECOGNIZING AND REWARDING EMPLOYEE CONTRIBUTIONS

In Chapter 8, we highlighted the significance of providing competitive compensation and benefits as a crucial retention strategy. Now, we delve into the power of recognizing and rewarding employee contributions as a potent tool in fostering a culture of loyalty and commitment. Acknowledging employees' efforts and achievements is not a mere formality; it is a genuine expression of appreciation that fuels their motivation and dedication to your organization.

The Impact of Employee Recognition:

Employee recognition is more than just a feel-good gesture; it has a profound impact on employee morale, job satisfaction, and overall engagement. When employees feel seen and valued, they are more likely to be proactive, enthusiastic, and invested in their work.

Creating a Culture of Appreciation:

Foster a culture where appreciation and recognition are woven into the fabric of daily operations. Encourage managers and peers to acknowledge contributions, both big and small, and celebrate individual and team successes.

Timely and Specific Recognition:

Recognition should be timely and specific, tying the acknowledgment to the particular achievement or behavior. This personalized approach demonstrates sincerity and reinforces the desired actions.

Peer-to-Peer Recognition:

Encourage peer-to-peer recognition as well. Employees often best understand the efforts and challenges faced by their colleagues, making their recognition meaningful and authentic.

Incentives and Rewards Programs:

Implement incentives and rewards programs that align with your organization's values and goals. These may include bonuses, gift cards, paid time off, or even experiences that employees cherish.

Celebrating Milestones and Achievements:

Mark milestones, work anniversaries, and significant achievements with celebrations and accolades. These occasions provide opportunities to show gratitude and reinforce the employee's impact on the organization.

Public Recognition:

Publicly acknowledge employee contributions through company-wide announcements, newsletters, or bulletin boards. Public recognition not only boosts the recipient's morale but also inspires others to strive for excellence.

Opportunities for Advancement:

Recognition can extend beyond verbal praise. Offer opportunities for career advancement, challenging projects, and leadership roles to employees who consistently excel.

Feedback as Recognition:

Constructive feedback can also be a form of recognition. When provided in a supportive manner, feedback shows employees that their growth and development are valued.

Measuring the Impact of Recognition:

Track the impact of recognition initiatives on employee engagement, satisfaction, and retention rates. Analyze data and feedback to identify which recognition strategies are most effective for your workforce.

Inspiring a Culture of Gratitude:

Encourage employees to express gratitude to one another for their support and collaboration. A culture of gratitude fosters a positive and supportive work environment.

Remember, recognition is not just a nice-to-have; it is a strategic imperative in cultivating a committed and loyal workforce. When employees feel appreciated and valued, they are more likely to be emotionally connected to your organization, stay motivated, and contribute their best.

In the next chapter, we will explore the essential role of fostering meaningful employee engagement. Engaged employees are the driving force behind organizational success, and organizations that prioritize engagement are rewarded with increased productivity and retention. Let us continue our journey to unlocking the secrets of employee retention together.

CHAPTER 10: FOSTERING MEANINGFUL EMPLOYEE ENGAGEMENT

In Chapter 9, we emphasized the power of recognizing and rewarding employee contributions as a key retention strategy. Now, we delve into the essential role of fostering meaningful employee engagement as a driving force behind organizational success. Engaged employees are not just satisfied with their jobs; they are emotionally connected to their work, enthusiastic about their contributions, and deeply committed to the organization's goals.

Understanding the Essence of Employee Engagement:

Employee engagement goes beyond mere job satisfaction. Engaged employees are passionate about their roles, driven to excel, and aligned with the company's mission and values. They actively contribute their creativity and energy to propel the organization forward.

Building a Foundation of Trust:

Trust is the bedrock of engagement. Foster a culture of transparency, open communication, and authenticity. When employees trust their leaders and feel that their voices are heard, they are more likely to be engaged and invested in their work.

Aligning Individual Goals with Organizational Objectives:

Help employees understand how their individual contributions impact the organization's success. Clearly communicate the company's mission and vision, and demonstrate how each employee plays a vital role in achieving those goals.

Encouraging Autonomy and Empowerment:

Empower employees to make decisions and take ownership of their work. Provide them with the resources and support they need to succeed, and trust them to find innovative solutions to challenges.

Creating Opportunities for Skill Development:

Offer opportunities for skill development and career growth. Engaged employees are eager to expand their knowledge and capabilities, and they value organizations that invest in their professional development.

Supporting Work-Life Integration:

Promote a healthy work-life integration that allows employees to excel both professionally and personally. Flexibility in work arrangements and supportive policies contribute to a positive work environment.

Recognizing and Celebrating Success:

Continuously recognize and celebrate individual and team successes. Acknowledging accomplishments reinforces desired behaviors and motivates employees to continue striving for excellence.

Seeking Employee Feedback and Input:

Regularly seek feedback from employees on their work experiences, challenges, and ideas for improvement. Act on the feedback to show that their input is valued and that their contributions shape the organization.

Promoting Collaboration and Teamwork:

Encourage collaboration and teamwork across departments and levels. Engaged employees thrive in a collaborative environment where they can leverage their strengths and contribute to collective achievements.

Measuring Employee Engagement:

Utilize employee surveys and feedback mechanisms to gauge engagement levels within your organization. Analyze the data to identify areas for improvement and monitor progress over time.

Leadership's Role in Driving Engagement:

Leaders play a pivotal role in fostering employee engagement. Lead by example, inspire teams, and create a supportive and inclusive culture that empowers employees to thrive.

Remember, employee engagement is not a one-time effort; it requires continuous attention and dedication. Engaged employees are more likely to stay loyal, committed, and motivated, leading to increased productivity and success for your organization.

In the next chapter, we will explore the importance of offering opportunities for work-life growth and advancement. Organizations that prioritize career development and advancement opportunities are rewarded with a talented and loyal workforce. Let us continue our journey to unlocking the secrets of employee retention together.

CHAPTER 11: OFFERING OPPORTUNITIES FOR WORK-LIFE GROWTH AND ADVANCEMENT

I n Chapter 10, we emphasized the significance of fostering meaningful employee engagement as a driving force behind organizational success. Now, we shift our focus to the essential role of offering opportunities for work-life growth and advancement as a powerful retention strategy. Employees are motivated to stay with organizations that invest in their career development and provide a clear path for advancement.

Embracing a Culture of Learning and Development:

Create a culture that values continuous learning and professional growth. Offer a wide range of learning opportunities, such as workshops, webinars, mentorship programs, and access to online resources. Employees who feel supported in their development are more likely to remain loyal and committed.

Individualized Career Development Plans:

Collaborate with employees to create individualized career

development plans that align with their aspirations and the organization's needs. These plans should outline the skills and experiences required for advancement, empowering employees to take charge of their career paths.

Offering Challenging Assignments and Projects:

Provide employees with challenging assignments and projects that stretch their skills and capabilities. Encourage them to step out of their comfort zones and take on new responsibilities, fostering a sense of achievement and growth.

Mentorship and Coaching Programs:

Implement mentorship and coaching programs that connect employees with experienced leaders within the organization. These programs provide guidance, support, and valuable insights into navigating career progression.

Promoting Internal Mobility:

Encourage internal mobility by promoting from within whenever possible. Create a culture where employees see opportunities for growth within the organization, reducing the temptation to seek external opportunities.

Transparent Career Paths:

Be transparent about career paths within the organization. Clearly communicate the skills, experience, and performance criteria required for advancement to each level. When employees understand the expectations, they can work towards their goals with clarity and determination.

Performance-Based Advancement:

Tie career advancement to performance and achievements. Reward employees who consistently excel in their roles and contribute to the organization's success with opportunities for growth.

Employee Recognition for Developmental Achievements:

Recognize and celebrate employees' developmental achievements, such as completing training programs, earning certifications, or mastering new skills. This positive reinforcement reinforces the value of their efforts and encourages further growth.

Supporting Career Transitions:

Be supportive of employees who wish to transition to different roles or departments within the organization. Encourage cross-functional collaboration and provide resources to aid in successful transitions.

Measuring Career Development Success:

Regularly assess the success of career development initiatives by tracking employees' progress, satisfaction with growth opportunities, and retention rates. Use this data to refine and enhance your strategies.

Remember, offering opportunities for work-life growth and advancement is a win-win strategy. Employees are motivated to stay with organizations that prioritize their development, while organizations benefit from a skilled and committed workforce.

In the next chapter, we will explore the crucial role of effective communication in fostering employee loyalty and trust. Open and transparent communication builds strong connections and demonstrates that employees are valued stakeholders in your organization's journey. Let us continue our journey to unlocking the secrets of employee retention together.

CHAPTER 12: THE POWER OF EFFECTIVE COMMUNICATION IN BUILDING EMPLOYEE LOYALTY

In Chapter 11, we emphasized the importance of offering opportunities for work-life growth and advancement as a potent retention strategy. Now, we delve into the crucial role of effective communication in fostering employee loyalty and trust. Communication is the lifeblood of any organization, and when done well, it builds strong connections, enhances collaboration, and demonstrates that employees are valued stakeholders in your organization's journey.

Transparent and Open Communication:

Transparency is the cornerstone of effective communication. Be open and honest with employees about the organization's goals, challenges, and decisions. When employees feel included and informed, they are more likely to trust leadership and remain engaged.

Active Listening and Feedback:

Listening is an essential component of communication. Encourage open dialogue and actively listen to employees' ideas, concerns, and feedback. Show that their input is valued, and be responsive to their needs.

Consistent and Timely Updates:

Regularly provide updates on important company developments and changes. Timely communication prevents rumors and misinformation, fostering a sense of stability and trust among employees.

Two-Way Communication Channels:

Establish two-way communication channels that enable employees to share their thoughts and ideas with leadership. Whether it's through town hall meetings, surveys, or suggestion boxes, create a culture that encourages employee participation.

Recognizing Employee Contributions Publicly:

Publicly recognize and celebrate employee contributions and achievements. Highlighting their successes not only boosts morale but also reinforces a culture of appreciation and recognition.

Communicating Career Development Opportunities:

Clearly communicate career development opportunities and growth paths within the organization. Employees should be aware of the skills and experiences required for advancement, empowering them to take proactive steps in their career journeys.

Sharing Organizational Successes and Challenges:

Share both successes and challenges with employees. Celebrate achievements as a team and acknowledge collective efforts. Similarly, address challenges transparently and collaboratively to build a sense of unity and purpose.

Crisis Communication and Support:

During challenging times, provide clear and empathetic communication to reassure employees. Keep them informed about the steps being taken to navigate through crises, and offer support to alleviate stress and uncertainty.

Cultivating a Culture of Respectful Communication:

Promote a culture of respectful and constructive communication at all levels. Encourage employees to express their ideas and opinions without fear of retribution. Respectful communication strengthens relationships and fosters trust.

Measuring Communication Effectiveness:

Assess the effectiveness of your communication efforts through employee surveys, feedback, and engagement metrics. Use the data to identify areas for improvement and tailor your communication strategies accordingly.

Remember, effective communication is not just about disseminating information; it is a strategic tool for building a positive and engaged workforce. When employees feel heard, valued, and well-informed, they are more likely to stay loyal and committed to your organization's mission.

In the next chapter, we will explore the significance of fostering a diverse and inclusive workplace. Embracing diversity and creating an inclusive culture are powerful retention strategies that attract top talent and create a thriving work environment. Let us continue our journey to unlocking the secrets of employee retention together.

CHAPTER 13: EMBRACING DIVERSITY AND INCLUSION FOR RETENTION SUCCESS

In Chapter 12, we emphasized the power of effective communication in building employee loyalty and trust. Now, we shift our focus to the critical role of fostering a diverse and inclusive workplace as a powerful retention strategy. Embracing diversity and creating an inclusive culture not only attracts top talent but also cultivates a thriving work environment where employees feel valued, respected, and empowered to reach their full potential.

The Value of Diversity and Inclusion:

Diversity goes beyond surface-level differences; it encompasses a wide range of perspectives, backgrounds, and experiences. Embracing diversity in all its forms enriches your organization by promoting creativity, innovation, and adaptability.

Building an Inclusive Culture:

Foster an inclusive culture where every employee feels like they belong, regardless of their background or identity. Create an environment that celebrates diversity and treats each individual with respect and dignity.

Diverse Hiring and Talent Acquisition:

Promote diverse hiring practices to attract a wide range of candidates. Implement blind recruitment techniques, diversify your recruitment sources, and ensure that job postings use inclusive language.

Providing Equal Opportunities:

Offer equal opportunities for growth, advancement, and development to all employees. Ensure that your performance evaluation process is fair and unbiased, promoting a level playing field for career progression.

Cultural Awareness and Sensitivity Training:

Invest in cultural awareness and sensitivity training for employees at all levels. These initiatives promote understanding and respect, reducing the likelihood of unconscious biases in the workplace.

Employee Resource Groups (ERGs):

Establish Employee Resource Groups that support diverse communities within your organization. ERGs provide a platform for networking, mentorship, and creating a sense of community.

Leadership Diversity and Representation:

Encourage diversity at leadership levels. Representation matters, and diverse leadership fosters an inclusive environment and serves as an inspiration to employees.

Addressing Microaggressions and Discrimination:

Proactively address and address microaggressions, discrimination, and inappropriate behavior. Foster a culture where employees feel comfortable reporting such incidents without fear of retaliation.

Diverse Perspectives in Decision-Making:

Include diverse perspectives in decision-making processes. Encourage input from employees with varied backgrounds and experiences to make well-rounded and informed choices.

Measuring Diversity and Inclusion Progress:

Regularly assess your organization's progress in promoting diversity and inclusion through metrics and surveys. Use the data to identify areas for improvement and take decisive actions to drive change.

Remember, a diverse and inclusive workplace is not just a moral imperative; it is a strategic advantage in attracting and retaining top talent. When employees feel valued, respected, and included, they are more likely to be loyal, engaged, and dedicated to your organization's mission.

In the next chapter, we will explore the importance of fostering a positive and supportive work culture. A thriving work culture is a magnet for talented individuals and a catalyst for employee retention. Let us continue our journey to unlocking the secrets of employee retention together.

CHAPTER 14: FOSTERING A POSITIVE AND SUPPORTIVE WORK CULTURE

In Chapter 13, we emphasized the significance of embracing diversity and inclusion as a powerful retention strategy. Now, we delve into the crucial role of fostering a positive and supportive work culture as a magnet for talented individuals and a catalyst for employee retention. A thriving work culture is the beating heart of any organization, where employees feel a sense of belonging, camaraderie, and purpose.

The Essence of a Positive Work Culture:

A positive work culture is one where employees feel motivated, empowered, and connected to their work and colleagues. It is a culture that prioritizes well-being, open communication, and recognition of achievements.

Prioritizing Employee Well-Being:

Invest in employee well-being initiatives that promote physical, mental, and emotional health. Encourage work-life balance, provide resources for managing stress, and foster a supportive environment for those facing personal challenges.

Embracing Flexibility and Work-Life Integration:

Embrace flexible work arrangements that accommodate employees' personal needs and responsibilities. A culture that supports work-life integration empowers employees to perform at their best, both in and out of the workplace.

Promoting a Growth Mindset:

Encourage a growth mindset within the organization, where employees are motivated to learn, adapt, and embrace challenges. Celebrate innovation and learning from failures as stepping stones to success.

Promoting Collaboration and Teamwork:

Create opportunities for collaboration and teamwork across departments and levels. A collaborative culture fosters a sense of unity, encourages knowledge-sharing, and fuels collective achievements.

Celebrating Milestones and Achievements:

Regularly celebrate both individual and team accomplishments. Acknowledging milestones reinforces a culture of appreciation and motivates employees to continue striving for excellence.

Encouraging Employee Autonomy and Empowerment:

Empower employees to make decisions and take ownership of their work. Autonomy fosters a sense of trust and responsibility, driving intrinsic motivation and job satisfaction.

Promoting Transparency and Open Communication:

Maintain transparent communication with employees about organizational decisions, changes, and goals. Openness builds trust and fosters a sense of inclusion among employees.

Recognizing and Addressing Burnout:

Be vigilant in recognizing signs of burnout among employees. Implement strategies to address burnout, such as workload adjustments, mental health support, and time off to recharge.

Leading by Example:

Leaders play a crucial role in shaping the work culture. Lead by example, demonstrating the values and behaviors you wish to see in your employees. Your actions set the tone for the entire organization.

Measuring Work Culture Effectiveness:

Regularly assess the effectiveness of your work culture through employee surveys, feedback, and retention rates. Use the insights to continuously improve and strengthen your organization's culture.

Remember, a positive and supportive work culture is the cornerstone of employee retention. When employees feel valued, engaged, and aligned with the organization's mission, they are more likely to stay loyal and committed to contributing their best.

In the final chapter, we will recap the key retention strategies we've explored and emphasize the importance of a holistic approach in retaining top talent. Let us continue our journey to unlocking the secrets of employee retention together.

CHAPTER 15: A HOLISTIC APPROACH TO EMPLOYEE RETENTION

T hroughout this book, we have explored various powerful strategies to retain top talent and build a loyal and committed workforce. Now, in this final chapter, we emphasize the significance of adopting a holistic approach to employee retention—one that combines all the key elements we've discussed into a cohesive and impactful retention strategy.

The Power of Synergy:

Just as a puzzle's pieces come together to form a beautiful picture, a holistic approach to employee retention leverages the power of synergy. Each element—competitive compensation, nurturing employee development, work-life balance, recognition, effective communication, diversity and inclusion, and a positive work culture—strengthens the others, creating a resilient and attractive workplace.

The Employee Value Proposition (EVP):

At the heart of this holistic approach is the Employee Value Proposition (EVP). Your EVP is the unique set of benefits, rewards, and opportunities your organization offers to its employees in exchange for their skills and dedication. An effective EVP communicates the value an employee receives from working with your organization, beyond just monetary compensation.

Emphasizing the Total Employee Experience:

Employee retention is not just about singular moments; it's about the entire employee journey. From recruitment to onboarding, career development, and daily work experiences, every touchpoint contributes to the overall employee experience. A holistic approach ensures that each interaction is positive, impactful, and aligned with the organization's values.

Listening and Adapting:

An essential aspect of a holistic retention strategy is listening to employees. Actively seek feedback and pay attention to their needs and aspirations. Regularly adapt your strategies based on this feedback to demonstrate that your organization is responsive and invested in their well-being.

Continuous Improvement and Innovation:

A holistic approach to retention is not static. It requires continuous improvement and innovation. Stay updated with the latest trends and best practices in talent retention, and be open to trying new approaches to enhance employee engagement and satisfaction.

Leadership as Role Models:

Leaders play a pivotal role in the success of any retention strategy. Lead by example, embodying the values and principles of the organization. Cultivate a leadership team that is invested in the well-being of their teams and demonstrates empathy and understanding.

Celebrating Retention Success:

As you witness the positive impact of your retention efforts, celebrate your successes! Recognize and acknowledge the collective effort that has led to increased employee satisfaction and reduced turnover. Celebrating achievements reinforces a culture of appreciation and motivates further efforts.

A Shared Responsibility:

Remember, employee retention is a shared responsibility across the organization. It involves HR, leadership, managers, and every employee. A collective commitment to creating a positive and engaging workplace is essential for long-term success.

In conclusion, a holistic approach to employee retention is a powerful investment in your organization's future. By combining competitive compensation, growth opportunities, work-life balance, recognition, effective communication, diversity and inclusion, and a positive work culture, you create an environment where employees are inspired to thrive and remain loyal.

Thank you for joining us on this journey to unlock the secrets of employee retention. As you implement these strategies, may your organization flourish with a dedicated and motivated workforce, driving your success to new heights. Embrace the power of retention, and your organization will reap the rewards of a thriving and committed team.

Epilogue: A Future of Retention Success

As we conclude our exploration of employee retention strategies, we envision a future where organizations thrive with dedicated and motivated teams, achieving new heights of success. The knowledge and insights shared in this book pave the way for a bright future—one where employee retention is not just a challenge to overcome but a strategic advantage to embrace.

In this future, organizations prioritize nurturing their talent, recognizing that employees are their most valuable assets. They create a culture that celebrates diversity and inclusion, where every individual feels valued, respected, and empowered to contribute their unique perspectives and talents.

In this future, competitive compensation is a given, but organizations go beyond the numbers. They offer opportunities for work-life growth and advancement, fostering an environment where employees are inspired to take charge of their careers and reach new heights.

In this future, effective communication is the backbone of success. Organizations establish a culture of transparency and openness, fostering trust and collaboration across all levels. Listening to employee feedback becomes second nature, guiding continuous improvement and innovation.

In this future, recognition becomes an integral part of the organization's DNA. Leaders and colleagues alike celebrate achievements and milestones, nurturing a culture of appreciation and motivating employees to excel further.

In this future, work-life balance is not a mere catchphrase, but a tangible reality. Organizations embrace flexibility and support employees in harmonizing their personal and professional lives, resulting in a happier, healthier, and more engaged workforce.

In this future, a positive and supportive work culture flourishes, where employees wake up eager to contribute, knowing they are part of something greater than themselves. Leaders lead with empathy and compassion, setting the stage for high performance and employee satisfaction.

In this future, employee retention is seen as a shared responsibility—a commitment that transcends departments and titles. The entire organization rallies together to create an environment where talented individuals are drawn, nurtured, and inspired to stay.

As we bid farewell, we extend our heartfelt gratitude to all who have embarked on this journey with us. Together, we have uncovered the secrets of employee retention, and armed with this knowledge, we step into a future where organizations thrive and employees flourish.

May this future be your reality—a future of retention success, where the synergy of competitive compensation, nurturing growth, work-life balance, recognition, communication, diversity and inclusion, and a positive culture creates an unstoppable force of employee loyalty and commitment.

Thank you for accompanying us on this transformative journey. The future of retention success awaits you. Embrace it, and watch your organization soar to new heights of excellence and prosperity. The power of retention is now in your hands.

Acknowledging the Journey:

As we look back on this transformative journey through the realm of employee retention, we take a moment to acknowledge the dedication and commitment of those who have embraced the power of these strategies. It is you—the visionary leaders, the compassionate managers, the enthusiastic HR professionals, and the passionate employees—who will bring about the future of retention success.

Your determination to create a workplace where employees feel valued, supported, and inspired is a testament to the importance you place on your organization's human capital. You recognize that attracting and retaining top talent is not a mere business objective; it is the very essence of building a thriving and sustainable organization.

By adopting a holistic approach to retention, you have harnessed the power of synergy. You understand that competitive compensation, growth opportunities, work-life balance, recognition, communication, diversity and inclusion, and a positive work culture are not isolated pieces but integral components that fortify one another.

Your commitment to fostering a diverse and inclusive workplace demonstrates a belief in the strength of varied perspectives and the power of unity. In embracing diversity, you have created an environment where every employee feels welcomed and encouraged to bring their whole selves to work.

By investing in employee well-being and career development, you have sowed the seeds of loyalty and dedication. Your employees feel empowered to chart their own paths, knowing that your organization values their growth and celebrates their achievements.

Your dedication to open and effective communication has built bridges of trust between leadership and employees. You have established a culture where ideas are shared, voices are heard, and collaboration is at the heart of decision-making.

Through recognition and celebration, you have cultivated a culture of appreciation—one that uplifts and motivates employees to continue exceeding expectations. Your acknowledgment of their hard work fuels their passion for excellence.

As we part ways, remember that the journey to retention success is not finite. It is an ongoing adventure—a commitment to continuous improvement and innovation. Stay vigilant in listening to your employees, adapting your strategies, and celebrating your successes.

With the knowledge and insights gleaned from this journey, you possess the tools to shape the future of your organization —a future where employee retention becomes an unparalleled strength, propelling you ahead of the competition and into the realms of greatness.

Thank you for embracing the power of retention, for believing in the potential of your employees, and for daring to create a workplace where loyalty, dedication, and innovation thrive.

May your future be one of retention success—a future where your organization stands tall as a beacon of excellence, fueled by the unwavering commitment of your exceptional workforce.

The future is now, and it is yours to create. Go forth with confidence and determination, for the journey of employee retention success begins with you.